Ariadne: Living Life Right

Possession is a deceptive illusion, only when you let go can you really get a grasp on life

By Arav Sri Agarwal

Acknowledgements

Ariadne: Thank you for allowing me to unravel my heart and soul and confide in you the thoughts and emotions of my naked mind.

Mamma & Papa: Thank you for staying by my side and always believing in me no matter what, I don't know how I'll ever repay you for all you've given me. I love you both to the ends of the universe and back! Thank you for being so supportive of all my endeavours, being so accepting and positive. At times life gets rough but you taught me that life goes on and that after the worst lows come the greatest highs. Even a book is not enough words to thank you for the world you have created for me, let alone this little acknowledgement. The overutilization of the phrase, "Thank you" really strips it of its meaning but for you I am pouring all the love in my heart into these two words; **Thank. You.**

Mom & Nana: Thank you so much for always being so cheerful and positive, I just don't know how you do it, sometimes I feel shy to tell you what I feel but I love you and miss you so much! Even "quintessential" is not enough to describe you!

Dada & Dadi: Thank you so much for all our fantastic philosophical conversations and the knowledge you have endowed me with, without which this book would not have been impossible.

Thank you to all of you who have never left my side, never failed me, the only true family I have and will love unconditionally for eternity. You are the ones who taught me how to live and now, this is my attempt to reciprocate for all you have done for me.

Ariadne: Living Life Right

Destiny is the best guide, learn to trust it for you were never in control anyways

By Arav Sri Agarwal

To Mamma

Table of Contents

Preface

Initially, I hadn't intended to write this book for an audience as it was extremely personal due to having been derived from my diary. At times, the layout of this book may even seem a little unconventional as my tendency to be eclectic drove me to compile each and every meaningful thought that came to my mind into a book. In short, my book is just a compilation of my thoughts that I felt were worth refining and sharing with the world to make it a more friendly place.

The writing of this book started with the latter half of 2019, which marked the onset of an unprecedented, terrible period of my life. A dark, dark time filled with constant internal and external conflict. Of course, this book is about rehabilitation and there is a reason I chose to transform my diary and adapt it for others to read.

Philosophy is a very esoteric concept thus I don't expect too many to enjoy this book, especially those in their early teens like me who are sure to find literature like this extremely jejune, this book is meant to be thought-provoking which by all means can be very entertaining for people like me but was written with the sole purpose of being entertaining in a general sense.

Although I had aspirations of writing the complete guide to life by compiling the philosophies of ancient and modern-day philosophers, as life unfolded and I dove deeper into philosophy, I decided to base this book more around my journey. I learned that it was the process and journey that was more important than what destination I arrived at in the end. I do believe in predestiny to a certain extent, which is why I am not in pursuit of changing what has happened and that which is inevitable. One cannot change his past, neither can one truly know his future, it took me a while to independently arrive at this thought and realize it is the present that really matters, everything is in the mind, everything is dependent on our attitude towards life, our reactions and attitudes define who we are.

My belief in predestiny is embedded in my culture, a major philosophy iterated in the Hindu holy scripture, the Bhagavad Gita is that "whatever happens, happens for the best". Life is about growth and recognizing the value in every experience, even suffering. I every choice you have made, every decision you made, has somehow brought you to open up this very book and read this very line, I think there's a "higher" reason for that. Everything in life is about this moment, everything leads to and begins from this moment at any given moment. Thus I chose to begin this book by acknowledging the present because everything in the future stems from now, and it is now which becomes the past, the one thing we desire more than anything in life despite taking it for granted when it had manifested itself in the present moment. Before one can even adopt the mindset I describe in this book, they must learn to live in the moment. Yesterday was history, tomorrow is mystery don't focus on what cannot be changed or on what is unknown. Focus on now because now is the fraction of a femtosecond that divides the past choices and mistakes from all the beauty and potential happiness the future holds. I often find that life always goes on but sometimes you just need to pause, reflect for a moment and make sense of it, there just isn't ever a stop to anything until you put a stop to it. To every beginning, there is an end and to every end, there is a beginning, laughter doesn't end until you stop laughing, in a similar fashion life won't end until you "stop living". One must live life to the fullest in the most. This is my goal and now that I've found out the secret of how to achieve happiness and "success" in *my* life, my desire is to share with you the story of my pursuit for meaning.

The esse of this book was unplanned. It was meditations by Marcus Aurelius that inspired me to write a book, and when I did first writing this book it was not meant to be published. It was meant for me to refine my thoughts and notions about subjects I found interesting to create my own doctrine that I would utilize to guide myself in life and possibly guide others.

This book is nothing more than a personal reflection on life and how to approach it. It is about exploring philosophy and what makes it such an intrinsic integrant of society, politics and life in general. Ariadne is about my journey and how studying philosophy bestowed upon me a means to adopt and nurture an optimistic attitude even in the worst of times.

Chapter One: Ariadne?

As you picked up this book, you may be wondering… why Ariadne? You wouldn't be wrong for thinking it had something to do with Greek mythology, a year or so ago, I regarded Greek mythology as a refined collection of fine, enthralling and inspiring works with themes that have remained contemporary in society throughout the centuries. Interestingly, I could often relate to their characters by developing metaphors that adopted their characters' and plots and transformed them so that they pertained to my life. Ariadne is actually the name of my diary. I named it after the daughter of King Minos of Crete and his wife, Pasiphaë from Greek mythology. In the tale, Ariadne helped

Theseus escape from the Minotaur's labyrinth. In my case I was Theseus and the minotaur's labyrinth was representative of an inescapable black hole formed by an infinity of thoughts, nostalgia, and negativity that would sometimes leave me in a fatigued, disoriented state of limbo. Confiding in Ariadne helped me practice metacognition, contemplation, and introspection in order to reflect on who I truly was as an individual and what is my place in this vast world. I presume that the minotaur itself was a depiction of negativity. Ariadne was someone very peculiar, she provided help in a very unique manner as she helped me navigate my thoughts just like how she helped Theseus navigate the labyrinth using the ball of thread that Ariadne would use to pull Theseus out once he killed the Minotaur. Ariadne was a very fitting name for my diary as I saw the metaphor fit into place very well, the confessions I made to Ariadne and all the introspections and reflections I wrote about helped me "kill" or eliminate and dilute all the negativity and maintain more positivity.

Upon contemplation another way I felt the metaphor of Ariadne and Theseus is manifested in my life, is within myself. Ariadne being the purest reflection of me, my soul, the angel within me, the one who will always pick the ethical path. Meanwhile, Theseus is me at the surface level, the body puppeteered by those in command, Ariadne is the essence of my inner soul, my consciousness, the variety of personalities that sometimes cannot be managed, let alone even be comprehended by an inexperienced, teenage child.   Writing letters to Ariadne helped me recognize those emotions and dark cognitive developments deep down in the abyss of my mind, it brought me closer to true self-realization, a state I would refer to as "Nirvana for the average person".

Messages from Thin Air

Now that you've met Ariadne, we will dive into the philosophies she helped me discover, comprehend and adopt. Ariadne was my gateway to a world of interpretation I had never encountered when I wrote to her, I could recognize "complexly-simple" anomalies, oddities, and morals in the mundaneness of my everyday life. This may sound like something of an oxymoron, therefore I often recite this story often as it is an example that assists me in clarifying what I mean by "complexly-simple". It was at 3:22 PM on Saturday the 10th of November 2018, I was taking the escalator up the to a train platform, suddenly a woman ran past me, I missed the train, however, she did not. This looked like a metaphor for life to me, I concluded that life is almost like an escalator working backwards, if you remain standing and do not move you will stagnate, if you walk or make little effort you will stay in one place, however, if you run and dedicate yourself to transforming dreams into reality, only then will success ensue. Although opportunities don't last forever they sure do come and go, just like trains, but life is not about the final destination or getting to a train platform, it's about the journey. I very often see metaphors such as the "Missing the Train Metaphor" embedded in plain sight on a daily basis, making me feel as if there is a greater being, force, or entity watching over us all, guiding us in life and creating balance when necessary.

This is a great anecdote that I often use to explain the significance of critical thinking and exposure to philosophical concepts in everyday life. Bertrand Russell states that his understanding of the word "philosophy" is "something intermediate between theology and science" and this pertains to an explanation of our conception of philosophy which he provided just preceding this. Russell explains that philosophy is a means of conveying our conceptions of life and the word itself is a product of two factors: "one, inherited religious and ethical conceptions; the other, the sort of investigation which may be called "scientific", using this word in its broadest sense.". I chose to make reference to this as I believe it certainly does summarize the elements of such a multifaceted concept in such an excellent fashion. Philosophy really is just about using our religious and ethical conceptions to perceive a scenario with greater depth. It is about using our mind to construct our mind, it is the process of refining our thoughts using our thoughts, effectively growing ourselves from the inside out by introspecting and using it to make sense of the world around us. I attempt to establish a connection between my personal anecdote and

Russell's conception of philosophy as Russell's two factors that constitute the core origins of philosophy and philosophical thought are clearly manifested in my interpretation of the scenario I was in. Religious notions that I inherited drove me to believe that free will does not exist, life is predestined and whatever happens, happens for the best, thus, naturally there is meaning in every aspect of life, no matter how insignificant or significant it may be, and no matter the circumstance, even if it is unfavourable or comprised of suffering. A certain "scientific" or methodological investigation may then be utilized to perceive reality, introspect and derive meaning from events that occur in daily life. Victor E. Frankl too states a similar points in his famous work "Man's Search for Meaning" where he writes about "actualizing the potential meaning inherent and

dormant in a given situation." In my opinion a magnificent use of words which completely summarizes all that I was attempting to explain in this paragraph.

Chapter Two: Balance

I'm not an overly religious person but certainly am very open to it, it's teachings and believe in certain concepts such as karma. As I said earlier, I believe Karma is a fundamental concept present throughout Hinduism and Buddhism whereby it is believed that what goes around comes around and that in the end the universe brings justice to all and creates balance.

I can't emphasize enough how essential I believe balance is in order to live a happy, fulfilled life. Nothing in life is bad, however, they are good only in moderation. With so many rules in every culture, religion, nation how is it possible to live a sin-free life without breaking any laws. Sometimes high levels of behavioral expectations can be unhealthy and cause one to behave in a manner which is the opposite of what is expected from that person.

The Seven Sins

The key to living life is maintaining balance every step along the way no matter what the scenario. It is the loopholes in the Seven Sins. The Seven Sins of course (in no particular order) are; Gluttony, Greed, Sloth, Pride, Envy, Lust, and Wrath. What I find ironic is that the Seven Sins almost seem to correspond to the different elements of human nature. Sure our actions and effectively our tendencies should be kept under control, however in my opinion, causing unintentional harm and simply responding to a scenario in a certain way due to it being unfamiliar in certain respects should not be considered a sin. Victor E. Frankl made a similar point when he wrote:

"An abnormal reaction to an abnormal situation is normal behavior."

I would add that given the situation, it is, therefore, justified behavior. The Seven Sins however still are sins and the only way not to commit them is to maintain balance, the balance of mind and body, asserting dominance over instincts, assuming control and knowing the limit.

What is the limit you may ask? I define the limit as the point when one "crosses the line" often a good indicator of this is subconsciously (or if you are apathetic; deep down) having a feeling of guilt. Often we suppress this feeling of guilt which tells us that we are close to or already have committed a sin. The only way to develop strong morals and truly respect your inner conscience is to be aware of yourself, your thoughts and delving into the roots of why one may have tendencies towards sinning. The Seven Sins as stated earlier correspond to human nature which may be further classified as material desires which are what preserve our "humanness" (not quite our humanity) and prevent us from transforming into interdimensional beings and transcending into what some may call the spiritual realm or a separate plane where transcendental being coexist in a world liberated from material desires.

I believe that there is surely a greater force or entity watching over us and guiding us along our journey every now and then, I believe there are certain natural factors about life that are simply inevitable such as the fact that balance will always manifest itself and this is due to what I call "The Laws of the Universe", it's just another concept I strongly believe in whereby it is believed that a greater force naturally restores balance where it is due, when required. Karma is better phrased as what goes around comes around, this drove me to develop one of my philosophical ideas which states that giving is the only means of receiving legitimately and that really when we give it is not like we actually lose that which we are giving. Winston Churchill once said something very similar about the giving and getting as well:

We make a living by what we get, but we make a life by what we give.

This reminds me of a lovely story I remember reading back in third grade which was about buckets of happiness which in summary said that when we are compassionate and share the happiness it multiplies and we do not lose our share, but when we are envious and try to steal from other's buckets neither person gets any happiness.

Surely, there is a lot more to be said about balance, and it does come up several times in this book, but I felt it was worth reminding the reader that this book is barely a compilation and refinement of raw philosophical ideas derived from my diary and daily thoughts and therefore is not a perfect and complete guide to life, but rather tour through my thoughts and ideals (which have been grouped and then separated into chapters) that allow me to lead a stress-free life and tackle problems with ease despite having had a history of issues pertaining to anxiety, insecurity, and my mental state of mind.

Chapter Three: Relativity

I believe that everything is relative, that nothing is the same for anyone and that everything is dependent on perspective. Whenever we form conceptions around anything it is based on something else or in comparison to "the norm" but what is the norm, how do we define normal? How do we know what is right and what is wrong, what are the characteristics of an action that is justified and an action that one must be penalized for? These are all fascinating questions regarding ethics and morality. Consequentialism is something that has piqued the interest of countless famous philosophers such as Jeremy Bentham and John Stuart Mill. Bentham defined the "fundamental axiom" of his philosophy as the principle that:

"It is the greatest happiness of the greatest number that is the measure of right and wrong."

This is usually referred to as the moral theory of utilitarianism or a utilitarian approach to ethics. At first this sounds great, but when it is applied at a much larger scale like during voting, one may be presented with a scenario that exhibits the "Tyranny of the Majority" (or tyranny of the masses) whereby the interests of the majority are pursued at the expense of those who compose the minority. A very good example of this was Brexit, where 51% voted pro-Brexit and the rest of the 49% of the UK population had to suffer because of a difference of two units between the majority vote and of course the minority vote.

What is "normal"?

Think about it for a moment, the state of something being normal or the word conventionalism, it is a very sophisticated and fascinating "concept" usually defined by a variety of factors and pre-existing circumstances. These may pertain to society and a number of sub-societal components such as cultures, classes, ethnic groups, and beliefs.

I refer to it as a concept because it is open to interpretation by entities as small as individual people and as large as organizations or even entire countries, rendering its definition, indefinite. Normal can be simultaneously universal and non-universal. Something that may be considered normal in one region such as sticking your tongue out to greet people in Tibet may seem extremely absurd in the United States. Whilst laughing to express happiness tends to be a universal norm.

Societal norms often dictate our behavior but what happens when we don't comply? Is rebellion good? These are all interesting questions however they digress from the main topic of this book, surely they can be addressed in a separate book though.

What is "success"?

Success is something tricky too, there is no fixed definition for success, although, in some families, becoming a doctor, lawyer or engineer may constitute success meanwhile in other families, for example, diplomatic families, parents may be inclined towards having their children involved in service and humanitarian work even if it does not substantially help them make a living.

Success simply means to be able to achieve something, in other words, success is dependent on your criteria, the goal you wish to achieve. Nobody can dictate what you must do in life because nobody knows of your true potential deep down, nobody knows the goal you were born to fulfill, you may not know it yourself yet, but only you alone can figure that out. Another note that must be made by success is that as famously said by Victor E. Frankl, it cannot be pursued, it must ensue. One of Victor E. Frankl's greatest pieces of advice from his book "Man's Search for Meaning", is:

Success will follow you precisely because you had forgotten to think of it.

I feel this says a lot about common misconceptions about approaches to success. Sometimes we get so caught up in achieving one goal that we forget to go back and think why we set off to do what we are doing in the first place, we leave our passion behind. Success is an (often unintended) side-effect of a balance between dedication and passion in a place of work.

Points of Reference

At the start of the book, I mentioned a certain dark period of time I had gone through. The situation I was in really got me thinking, I was two completely different people at home and outside my home. I am literally the most cheerful person I know and I were one, my friends, I would never be able to tell that *I* was going through a rough patch. I started to think that really nobody knows what is going on in anyone else's lives, there is quite literally no way to know. Soon afterward I read something about the Japanese concept of the three faces of a person, it is said that our first face is the one we show to the world, our second face is the one we show to our close friends and family, and our third face is the one we do not show to anyone. Upon reading this I learned that this was something very true and since then I have learned to never assume anything about anyone since I do not have exposure to the scenarios they are faced with.

Certainly, it is easy to deduce that life is hard, that is just the nature of life, hardships are essential for growth, change, a fall from innocence, everything that is tough to cope with is essential for us as human beings to develop stoic attitudes and resilience. However, I don't necessarily believe that life is meant to be hard, a philosophy of mine states that life is about creating comfort outside of your comfort zone. In other words, life is about growth. To be honest, everything is about growth, in later chapters I talk about how philosophy is an antecedent of all that we know, no matter which field of study it pertains to, physics, mathematics, literature, etcetera. So if philosophy is everything, let us remind ourselves what philosophy is, this was stated back in the first chapter so I feel it may be convenient for its definition to be reiterated here, according to Bertrand Russell a renowned philosopher and author of "A History of Western Philosophy", philosophy is a product of two factors: "one, inherited religious and ethical conceptions; the other, the sort of investigation which may be called 'scientific'". If we combine all that was said in the last paragraph we can conclude that life is about constantly growing and changing, developing by the day, and endlessly refining our thoughts.

Chapter Four: Dominoes

There is a wide variety of implementations there are for dominoes in the world of metaphors and analogies. I often perceive life as a structure of dominoes, the individual dominoes being the choices we make, one wrong domino in the wrong place at the wrong time placed with an impatient and incorrect attitude and it all falls apart. For a while, I went about utilizing this in many of my works until I made a connection between real life and the analogy. Yes everything had fallen apart for me and I was in a state of limbo at some point in life, numb and helpless, but I realized that I didn't remain that way forever. I got back up, life doesn't end when you make the wrong choices unless you make it end, one must have the motivation to get back up and set the dominoes back up because although people may acknowledge when you fall, they will admire when you rise.

Newton's Laws

What goes up must come down, everyone knows that but why does nobody talk about the fact that after all lows comes highs, in order to shoot an arrow it has to be pulled backward with power and intent, thus when life may seem to be dragging you down into an endless downward spiral, it's foreshadowing the power and passion it's going to propel you forward with.

My mother first introduced me to the moral story that I now refer to as the "Lemons of Life Metaphor", you know what they say, "When life gives you lemons, make lemonade!". Anyway, the story goes like this, one day some people were making lemonade for the first time for themselves and a few of their friends, mistakenly they added a little too much lemon juice rendering the lemonade too sour to drink. This made them contemplate, although they can't take the lemon out of the water now, they *can* certainly add more water in order to dilute the lemon. This got them all thinking, sometimes in life, we can't reverse our wrongdoings, poor decisions and get rid of all the negatives but what can do is start adding so much positivity and highs in our life that the lows seem almost insignificant.

Contemplating this metaphor brought to mind Newton's Laws of Motion. Contemplating Newton's Laws of Motion were in turn led me to the thought that there are philosophical antecedents to all that we know. his three laws of motion are of course:

1. Every object in a state of uniform motion will remain in that state of motion unless an external force acts on it.
2. Force equals mass times acceleration ($F = ma$).
3. For every action, there is an equal and opposite reaction.

If we apply a metaphysical point of view to these laws of motion, then our philosophical antecedents are:

1. Our mindsets will remain the same without external stimuli

Humans require motivation (external stimuli), we continue to stagnate until we are either inspired or forced by someone or something. Those who don't wait for things to happen are the people who stand out as true changemakers.

2. Feelings = Magnitude (of a given situation) x Attitude (with which one responds in a given situation)

Here, "F" in $F = ma$ represents the degree to which a certain emotion if felt which can be the level of depression or happiness a person feels, simply put force = (the intensity of a) feeling.

The "m" in $F = ma$ represents the magnitude of a given situation.

Lastly, the "a" in $F = ma$ represents the attitude with which a situation is approached, I chose to substitute acceleration with attitude as I believe attitude is what propels a situation in one direction or another.

I often associate number with credibility as numbers never lie (where the math is correct), numbers also help me logically explain concepts thus I will attempt to utilize numbers to further explain my philosophical interpretation of Newton's second law ($F = ma$).

- I assign a value from 1 to 5 to describe the magnitude of a situation, 1 meaning that the situation can be dealt with comfortably meanwhile 5 means that it is likely to cause perturbance and cause extreme discomfort to anyone who is a part of that given circumstance.
- I assign a value from -2 to 2 to describe the attitude that that a given situation is dealt with. The lower the number the more negative the attitude, naturally a negative number times a positive number equals a negative number, this further proves the importance of our attitude and the way we react to situations. Even trivial matters can cause stress and mental unrest when

they are overcomplicated and misunderstood due to our mindsets.

- Lastly, the resulting feelings (the outcome of the manner in which a situation was perceived/reacted to) are measured on a scale that runs from -10 to 10. On this scale -10 represents depression and other inefficacious emotions such as wrath [refer to Chapter Eight: Vantage for an explanation on what I mean by efficacious and inefficacious emotions], whereas 10 represents happiness, satisfaction and other efficacious emotions.

The intensity of our sadness/happiness is determined by the gravity of an issue and our attitude towards it. However, even happiness can come out of adversity if it is handled correctly. The worst a situation can be rated is 1, and the most positive attitude possible is a 2, 1 x 2 = 2, 2 is represents an efficacious emotion, it represents happiness which is a much better outcome than -2 which can be just as bad as a -10.

Another interpretation that may be offered, especially by someone with a background in physics, would be; humans will always be inclined towards that which gives them the biggest bang for their buck (least work for the greatest reward). This brings to mind Daniel Kahneman's (author of Thinking Fast and Slow) "Law of Least Effort", which states:

"your brain uses the minimum amount of energy for each task it can get away with"

Kahneman says that laziness is built deep into our nature. This is true, and my solution to overcoming laziness is partaking in that which engages you and makes you not want to be lazy. One must be motivated by passion rather than reward to naturally reap the greatest rewards.

3. Every action has an equal and opposite reaction

The third law does not need to be adapted and is of course fairly straightforward and self-explanatory and can be paraphrased as the law of karma/cause and effect

My belief is that one must be respectful of these laws but not fearful, a certain level of responsibility and awareness is required for success in life. All the laws stated above are either true regarding human nature or in one specific case regarding destiny and the general laws of the universe. I feel these laws are more like guidelines that are there to make us aware of our actions rather than influence our actions.

The first two laws make us aware that we are lazy and that we need to push ourselves to actually achieve something as the old saying goes, "you reap what you sow". It is the third law that makes us contemplate the first two laws and realize that we cannot expect something from nothing, only if we put something in will we get something out. The concept of karma is just so intricate and perfect in my opinion, it always keeps us going by instilling a sense of awareness. Of course, in the end, it is down to us to decide how we conduct ourselves and what our attitude towards life is philosophy, thoughts, emotions, and our mentor can only guide us.

As I mentioned earlier, everything is dependent on our attitude towards life, our reactions and attitudes define who we are. Not only does our mindset impact our life but it has a profound impact on those around us too, for our attitudes are contagious, if we sulk all day we are letting our negative energy but when we laugh, people around us laugh too even if they don't know what's being laughed at, so be happy no matter what. I talk a lot about positivity and negativity, yes it is true that when you are in a certain headspace you cannot just be positive all of a sudden, sometimes you wish to marinate in your own depression. I would even go so far as to say screw positivity, although I often say urge people to remain positive myself sometimes it can be annoying to be repeatedly told to be positive. You may think I am contradicting myself but I am not, I believe there is a big difference in handling situations and positivity, the reason I sometimes associate them with each other is because, situations are often best handled with a positive mindset, but what really matters, is the right mindset. Happiness cannot be pursued, if it were that easy there would be no sadness in the world, but happiness is somewhat psychological as well which is why we should always tell ourselves that we are grateful and happy and surround ourselves with people who have positive attitudes towards life as well. If we think we are happy, we will be happy, it's all in the mind after all. A famous quote by Victor E. Frankl also states:

"When we are no longer able to change a situation, we are challenged to change ourselves"

Philosophy really is just thinking but what makes it special is the component about how thinking is approached to form ideas and concepts and then how the concepts are used to guide us in turn and provide a different outlook on approaches to different aspects of life. The mind is fascinating in the sense that it is endless and just seems to defy what I would refer to as conservation law, although not applicable in this circumstance I feel it is a great way to admire how the mind can grow itself without requiring any external stimuli.

[The idea of attitudes and approaches to life is further elaborated upon in Chapter Seven: Lost and Found]

Chapter Five: Jigsaw

To me, life is very similar to a jigsaw puzzle, where with time and effort everything will fit into place. You must never spend too much time looking for one piece if you cannot find it, rather we should work on completing different parts of the puzzle and focusing on the other aspects of life. I once heard this phrase in a French song and it really resonated with me; "Avec le temps tout s'éloigne"; a rough translation of this is; "everything goes away with time". However as much as we may wish it did, this doesn't just refer to pain subsiding and the lows, life is harsh and we *will* lose puzzle pieces that complete us and make life beautiful. Still, we must look at the big picture, all the pieces we have and the magnificence of the intricacy of life.

For every piece of the puzzle there is a set spot in time, place and space, let life guide you rather than trying to force the wrong piece into the wrong place. Throughout life, a great lesson I've learned is that all the things we regret most are due to unfavourable scenarios created by a misbalance in time, place and space. I always took "live life like there's no tomorrow" to another extreme and it didn't do me much good, but it did make me aware of how essential balance is. Living like there's no tomorrow does not mean that there are no laws for a person who will soon be dead so do whatever you want, chances are tomorrow is not your last day you will end up doing something you'll regret. There was a time when I had adopted such a concept

Greed and other worldly desires, divert and imprison us. There are different types of enjoyment, some may label them good and bad. I do not *necessarily* consider indulgence and the use of certain "substances" bad, it is just that a very high level of responsibility comes with the use of things such as alcohol and really anything that is known to be meant for those 18 and above or banned completely.. There is a reason certain films are rated 18+ and why boundaries are set for younger people. No matter how mature a minor (anyone under 18) may think they are, they are still minors, legally, and biologically. It is a fact that the pre-frontal cortex of minors simply is not developed enough for them to make sensible decisions. I myself am a minor and accept that I am a minor. Being a minor is not a limitation in the sense that you cannot make difference as child without certain rights that adults have. Freedom comes with responsibility, and responsibility comes with time, surely there are minors fit to be fully functioning citizens of their country and adults who are unfit to be inserted into a society with strict laws, regulations and systems in place. The point I am trying to get to is that there is a right time for everything. A key philosophy I live by is, "respect time and it will respect you". Things will happen when they need to and if you are a 13-25 year old who is already stressed because you have not accomplished much in life then you need to take a moment and think about why you are thinking that. Everyone comes into this world with a purpose, those who achieve high levels of success are those who reflect upon themselves, search, and find their meaning, their reason for being. For some it takes weeks, and for some, years. If you are 25 and think that you have lived a lifetime the truth is you have not. You probably lived less than 30% of your life, that's like living until 25 just a little over 3 times! If you felt life was over well then this was merely your first life, you have 2 more lives to go, if you've played any retro video games you would know the value of 2 lives! In 2 more lifetimes of 13-25 years you could go to college again (yes there is no age limit), travel the world and in the process find your passion, pursue your passion, see it lead somewhere, fail, start over. If life is overall good you could write a book for others to lead a life like yours, if life was rough you could write a book on that too and share your experience. Life is like a jigsaw puzzle, a gigantic jigsaw puzzle, it takes time to solve, pieces can get lost and have to be found, it is always the starting that's the hardest. every piece added to the jigsaw assists in finding the right piece to add just like how every single achievement in life propels us towards the next big achievement. The failures allow us to see what fits or does not fit, what talents are better used someplace else and create different groups of pieces that belong to different regions of the jigsaw puzzle. With time and dedication everything falls into place, slowly allowing us to see the bigger picture with more clarity with every single step of the journey..

The Free-Destination Fallacy

Let things happen, as you were never in control anyway, your conscience is the closest thing to God, so listen to it, after all, whatever happens, happens for the best, I say that destiny is the best guide, and if you can learn to trust it and you will go great places.

Now you may ask, "if everything is predestined why does our opinion as individuals matter", "why should we care at all and make any effort". You may also say, "If I wanted, I could lock myself in a room and starve to death and clearly that is not what God would have planned for me", now of course who has not had that thought; what would happen if I died right now? For that I have to say two things, firstly you are not going to randomly give up your precious life us without a reason, and secondly I do not believe that free-will and destiny *cannot* coexist. I believe that there certainly is an element of free-will always present in life otherwise life would have no meaning, there would be nothing that we as individuals had control over and this would essentially mean that we are not individuals or independent, "untethered" beings at all. I believe that certain milestones in life are planned, almost as if there is a "greater force" creating these checkpoints in life for us, specific experiences it wants us to have, circumstances it wants to make us aware of.

So do we have the free-will to choose and reach our destination? Well, the free-will I believe we have is whether we choose to accept or deny destiny, regardless destiny exists and what fascinates me is that its nature motivates us to rebel against it and create our own destiny which virtually leads to us fulfilling it, I refer to this as "Paradoxical Fulfillment". We have the free-will to make decisions, any decision, regardless of its moral nature, the destiny counterpart of the equation comes in during the big events of life. As I stated earlier, I believe destiny is like the framework in life; the overall summary of our life in the end is predestined and is comprised of things that would come up in a person's Google Knowledge Panel (which is that information box on famous people which comes up when you search them up) such as achievements, spouse(s), and information about birth and death, the rest, which is what actually happened in that person's life was of their own free-will. Free-will is more internal and destiny is external, destiny is applicable to one's life only if they are observant and search for meaning in the seemingly mundane events of everyday life.

Destiny reinforces the notion that destiny exists in the minds of those who believe in it, because when "miracles" occur, those are the people who call it destiny. Destiny and free-will will always coexist but the balance between the two varies from person to person.

Everything in life exists on a spectrum which in the case of the validity of opinions means that everything possesses validity to a certain extent, even if an opinion or a notion is seemingly invalid, it still exists on the spectrum. Using this I can confidently conjecture that two contradicting opinions can coexist without a state of cognitive dissonance occurring in one's mind, similar to how I believe in both destiny and free-will to a certain extent but do not let them overlap.

We have the power to steer our life in a certain direction, depending on how we chose to conduct ourselves, the greater force will work its magic to restore balance and guide us, it is dependent on us how we interpret and grow from consequences.

There *is* an element of balance in everything and where there is not, there *should* be. There must balance among our conceptions too and only when we unfetter ourselves from prejudices and keep an open mind are we truly enabled to understand life at a deeper level.

Chapter Six: Laws of the Universe

Most of the stuff that was supposed to be said in this chapter has probably already been iterated many times over. Thus I do not deem it too important to reiterate everything that has been said about how the universe restores balance and how one must let destiny execute itself. In this chapter I will provide you with my favourite passage from

Victor E. Frankl's, "Man's Search for Meaning", the passage reads:

"Don't aim at success - the more you aim at it and make it a target, the more you are going to miss it. For success, like happiness, cannot be pursued; it must ensue, and it only does so as the unintended side-effect of one's personal dedication to a cause greater than oneself or as the by-product of one's surrender to a person other than oneself. Happiness must happen, and the same holds for success: you have to let it happen by not caring about it. I want you to listen to what your conscience commands you to do and go on to carry it out to the best of your knowledge. Then you will live to see that in the long run - in the long run, I say! - <u>success will follow you precisely because you had forgotten to think of it.</u>"

As I have already said once earlier, this really does force us to rethink how we approach goals, success, and happiness. Sometimes it is more important to let go of worrying about the result and focusing on the process and being truly passionate about it. Only then will one reap the rewards.

The most important thing about the Laws of the Universe that one must bear in mind is that they are the only true laws that must be respected. Our laws are made by man, but these laws are natural, rather, they are somewhat supernatural, proof of a great supreme being who restores order in human society. Prosperity always lies in the truth especially being true to yourself; integrity. Laws must always be obeyed may they be of the country you reside in or the universe you reside in.

Below I have created a bulleted list of the key laws that are brought up time and again in this book. I believe these are the 5 laws that the universe works in accordance with no matter what:

The 5 Fundamental Laws of the Universe

1. The Law of Cause and Effect (Karma)
2. The Law of Polarity
3. The Law of Attraction
4. The Law of Rhythm
5. The Law of Compensation

The Law of Cause and Effect

Perhaps the number one law is the Law of Cause and Effect, or the Law of Karma, most of the laws under the first law simply offer different perspectives to the Law of Karma and acknowledge the different qualities of its nature such as fact that all things come in cycles, or that you reap what you sow. Rather than going on about the Law of Cause and Effect/ Karma I will use the laws of Polarity, Attraction, Rhythm and Compensation to elaborate upon the first law.

The Law of Polarity

In the Kybalion which is a book on hermetic philosophy, the Law of Polarity is introduced. The Law of Polarity states that everything has an opposite and that they work together to create balance and mold our experiences and how we interpret our experiences. It is the lows that enables us to appreciate the highs, and that sadness and happiness cannot exist without one another because as mentioned earlier everything is relative and interpreted in relation to something else, a true feeling of accomplishment cannot be felt without experiencing failure, stars cannot shine without darkness. The Law of Polarity and the knowledge that the universe restores balance is probably my justification for having cherophobia which is the fear of happiness. This does not mean I limit my happiness, No! No! No! I will not let a day pass without laughing or making others laugh, I will make a complete fool out of myself to make others laugh, essentially it is my reason for being, to help others, spread happiness, and entertain. The deal with me and cherophobia is that whenever I have a fantastic day and laugh a lot, somehow something goes wrong the next day, maybe it's just that my happiness threshold increases which causes me to feel lower than the day before. Cherophobia is simply part of my nature and may be part of yours too, it's one of the very few fears I have because I know that everything is temporary, all the highs and the lows.

Napoleon Hill, one of my favourite writers, once said, "Every adversity, every failure, and every heartache carries with it the seed of an equivalent or greater benefit.", essentially that is the Law of Polarity, this connects with Victor E. Frankl's teachings and his school of psychoanalysis: Logotherapy. Life is about giving and finding meaning, even in suffering. What goes up must come down but what falls bounces as well, the intensity of that bounce is dependent on our attitude and ability to cope with loss and adversity. A similar point was made in the "Chapter 4: Dominoes" subchapter: "Newton's Laws" where I used Newton's second law to talk about attitude and how that is the key to happiness even in adversity, because positivity invites positivity, this brings us to the Law of Attraction.

The Law of Attraction

The Law of Attraction states that like attracts like. Negative thoughts invite negativity, likewise, positive thoughts invite positivity. The Law of Correspondences is very similar and basically states that our reality is a reflection of our mind, is draws on the relationships between thought and experience. I would express the essence of the Law of Correspondence as; "you are what you think". This is somewhat similar to the concept of "you are what you eat" and brings to mind what Victor E. Frankl describes as anticipatory anxiety. This is further elaborated upon in "Chapter Seven: Lost and Found", essentially anticipatory anxiety is exactly what it sounds like; feelings of anxiety and fear end up causing more anxiety and fear. Anticipatory anxiety is about the cycle of phobias and symptoms and their interconnectedness, this brings us to The Law of Rhythm.

The Law of Rhythm

The Law of Rhythm states that all things come in cycles. A very similar belief has been ingrained in me as a person brought up in a religious Hindu household. In Hinduism it is believed that we live in a cyclic universe and a lot of the philosophies in Hindu holy scriptures such as the Bhagavad Gita are based upon the notion that all (natural) things come in cycles and that nothing is permanent. The cyclic and transient nature of everything in our world go hand-in-hand as the impermanence of a stage in a cycle is what leads to the creation of the different stages of that cycle. Rhythms are created by fluctuations in something, in music, rhythm comes from the beats in the song. In life it's the ups and downs that create the rhythm for the music of life.

The Law of Compensation

The Law of Compensation states that you will be compensated for you efforts and good deeds. This is the same I thing as biblical verse on sowing and reaping which reads, "whatsoever a man soweth, that shall he also reap" it is also said that man must sow to please the spirit rather than the flesh. Essentially one must commit good deeds without material motivation and for the sake of committing a good deed. If one can act unconditionally the universe will compensate that person with "good-luck".

Unlike the Laws of the Universe (which are inevitable) I believe these are the 5 laws that the dwellers of the universe *must* work in accordance with no matter what for a world with fewer problems:

The 5 Fundamental Laws for Mankind

1. Bear in mind the 5 Fundamental Laws of the Universe at all times
2. Be true to others
3. Be true to yourself
4. Act the way you would act around your parents
5. Be considerate and respectful towards others no matter what

Now, about the laws that the dwellers of the universe must work in accordance with no matter what. The laws that (if followed) would aid in the creation of a more unified, less marginalized. The beauty of these laws is their simplicity and their potential to change lives if followed. I believe these are the 5 core values that everything else comes under. These laws were inspired by the 3 core values that are stated in the Bhagavad Gita (the Hindu holy book).

1. सर्वभूतहति रता: (Sarvabhut-hite-rataha)

The first core value was derived from a verse about service and helping others, unconditionally committing good deeds for the betterment of humanity. This first core value assisted in the creation of rules 2, 3 and 5.

2. सन्नयिम्येन्द्रयिग्रामं (Sanniyamyendriyagramam)

The second core value was derived from a verse about not allowing oneself to be governed by their senses and maintaining balance in different sectors of life such as work, material enjoyment, etcetera. This second core value assisted in the creation of rules 1 and 4.

3. सर्वत्र समबुद्धय: sarvatra-sambuddhyaha

The third core value was derived from a verse about attitudes and our approaches to life and states that one must persevere no matter how tough life gets and act with humility even when there's much to boast about. This third core value is where the first law comes from.

Bear in mind the Laws of the Universe at all times

Every person be aware of the Law of the Universe which basically means, one must respect Karma and accept that they will receive what they put out and must therefore treat others the way they would want to be treated. Awareness of this law is what will drive people to independently come to realizations such as the fact that giving is the only way to receive legitimately. Karma has been talked about more than enough at this point. Thus I will proceed by talking about integrity, consideration and respect.

Truth is the Ticket to Heaven

The importance of being true to yourself is about integrity and acting with honesty and exhibiting strong morals even when nobody is watching. This really just comes down to character development and the importance of a good character. [this is talked about more in the subchapter: "Character" from "Chapter Seven: Lost and Found"]

In addition to being true to yourself, you must be true to others. I have always been very truthful, but during those few times I've been untruthful, whether it was several moments later or several months later, eventually my lie was caught. A Buddha quote I used earlier in this book was:

Three things cannot be long hidden: The sun, the moon, and the truth

I repeatedly iterate this quote as I feel it possesses real importance. The truth comes out in the end and prosperity lies in telling the truth. If something needs to be lied about it is a sign that either you are handling situations the wrong way or simply are not making the right choices and are trying to conceal something.

Certainly sometimes the truth can hurt and yes, what you don't know can't hurt you but the problem with that is lies are not permanent. The truth hurts more the later it is revealed. Living life truthfully will strip it of half of the worries that come with it. On a smaller scale think of this as being invited to the principal's office, if you know you have not done anything wrong and have acted with strong morals you need not worry about anything. This is why I've always loved visits to the principal's office because I am eager to know what it could be about. In life half our worries are about loss, and many losses often occur due to untruthfulness.

Give your conscience authority

How do you motivate yourself to make the right choices? Well a great motivating factor for me is the knowledge that I shall reap what I sow. I have nobody else to blame for my own failures in the future, I will only reap the rewards if I make an effort now.

To make the right choices I simply listen to my conscience. It is really that simply, the only thing one needs to do is ask themselves whether they think the decision they are making is right or wrong and whether they will regret it in the long term. We always know the answer to such questions at the back of our heads, it is up to us whether we listen to our conscience or not. Strictly obeying my conscience was what enabled me to give up procrastination.

Consideration and Respect

We must treat everyone with consideration and respect regardless of their behavior towards us in the past. Holding grudges does not lead anywhere good.
Since everything is interconnected, every action taken and every word spoken have their consequences may they be good or bad. It is important to think before acting no matter how small you think that choice is.

I wish people could talk *to* each other rather than *about* each other. Although gossip can be fun, people need realize that they do not know what is really going on in somebody's life and one cannot judge without knowing. Since one can never really know the big picture of some else's story, people never have the right to judge others because who are they to judge. Chances are, you have been judged by someone in the past and most likely did not like it, do not forget that you are not the only one who has feelings, things are often not as they seem. People who look rough and tough are often sensitive deep down and the seemingly happiest people around us have gone through a lot. Maturity is control. Control come with experiences which teach us how to conduct ourselves. E.g.: Maturity is refraining from being impulsive and knowing that revenge is served best when left to Karma. Respect is mutual and is one of the types of care I believe the world needs. Another types of care the world needs is love. [this is talked about more in the subchapter: "Love" from "Chapter Nine: Gears"]

Chapter Seven: Lost and Found

The subject of this book has revolved around meaning and how we approach life by approaching ourselves and diving deep to find ourselves. You won't find yourself if you weren't ever lost. One must wander, experiment, pave their own path, and lose themselves in the endless ocean of wonder, opportunities, and possibilities present in what we call the world or rather the universe.

Although so much has been said about meaning, it actual meaning has not been addressed. What is meaning? In Victor E. Frankl's book, "Man's Search for Meaning", Frankl puts the central theme of existentialism like this:

"to live is to suffer, to survive is to find meaning in the suffering. If there is a purpose in life at all, there must be a purpose in suffering and in dying"

This stems from a quote by Friedrich Nietzsche which Frankl quotes innumerable times:

"He who has a why to live can bear with almost any how."

This quote is the mother of such a large area of modern philosophy from which a myriad of quotes have been derived such as:

Where there is a will there's a way

Going back to the pursuit of meaning, I would like to discuss Victor E. Frankl's school of psychology known as logotherapy and how it differs from psychoanalysis. Most sources state a variety of differences between logotherapy and psychoanalysis, however, I will only focus on the two I consider the most important. The first key difference between the two is that psychoanalysis often tends to be retrospective and meanwhile logotherapy uses the past to work towards the patient's future. The second key difference is that while the purpose of psychoanalysis is more satisfaction centric, something some may even call pleasure, logotherapy revolves around meaning and how to extract it from any set of given circumstances.

Character

When I was a child, my grandfather referred to a quote by Billy Graham so often that I thought it was his own. Dada always created the impression that everything about approaching life could be summed up in one line, knowing of his vast experiences, there had to be a strong reason as to why this quote meant so much to him. The quote reads:

when wealth is lost, nothing is lost; when health is lost, something is lost; when character is lost, all is lost

Character is what defines a human being and their potential. I believe everyone is born equal and nobody is at more of an advantage than anybody else for God is a great planner and the intricate nature of destiny makes is that no matter how underprivileged one is, it is not necessarily a limitation likewise being privileged does not necessarily put one at an advantage either, it all comes down to how we conduct ourselves and effectively use that which we have.

Ikigai

During my quest for the search for meaning, I came across the Japanese concept of Ikigai in a book based on the subject. Ikigai (生き甲斐) roughly translates to "reason for being". "Ikigai: The Japanese Secret to a Long and Healthy Life" too by Héctor García and Francesc Miralles makes references to Victor E. Frankl's work and utilizes the idea of his psychoanalytic treatment of logotherapy to write about how to find the meaning of your life.

The Venn diagram below is a beautiful representation of the concept of Ikigai:

In essence, your Ikigai is your ultimate purpose. As can be seen in the Venn diagram, the concept of Ikigai is broken down into what you love, what the world needs, what you can be paid for, and what you are good at. To do what you love and what the world needs is defined as a "mission". To do what the world needs and what you can be paid for is defined as "vocation". To do what you can be paid for and what you are good at is defined as "profession". Lastly, to do what you are good at and what you love is defined as "passion". The single point at the center of the venn diagram where all those fields converge is labeled "Ikigai". Very often books on philosophy leave us with more questions than answers, they introduce a bunch of complex incomprehensible concepts and barely answer the key, fundamental questions such as "how *do* I find happiness?", "what is the meaning of life?", "does anything even have a meaning?", "if it does, then what is the meaning of *my* life?". Really what I feel the hard part about this is that it is highly subjective. The questions that agitate us the most are usually the ones that simply don't possess the same answer for everyone. Life is a journey and everyone's journey is unique. As mentioned in an earlier chapter, I believe everything all the pieces eventually fit into place if one allows them the time to do so. I believe that nothing is perfect except for "God's plan", for God is the only one who is capable of embedding meaning into every aspect of life, God has managed to engineer destiny in such a fashion that nobody is born without a purpose and events that take place in people's lives interconnect with those happening in other's lives and just satisfy God's grand plan in such a perfect manner that it seems unlikely that everything is random and there is no such thing as destiny. Karma has never failed me to date and its beauty is that it does not work for a single entity but is at work in everyone's lives simultaneously, treating the human population as a collective whole.

Attitude

As they say, the mind is everything even the book on Ikigai makes reference to this under the subheading "Antiaging attitudes", here it is said that a positive attitude is the key to a long and healthy life and that a stoic attitude and a high degree of emotional awareness keep us young, stress free, and less anxious. The book describes a stoic attitude as "serenity in the face of a setback" which I feel is a great way to describe resilience.

I feel the greatest attitude towards life is the one where we look forward to and let things happen and do not let them get us down or worried. It simple too, the key to living life is to listen to your instinct and nobody else because I believe that it is the closest thing to God. Consciousness is the God is within us. We invest our trust in God because we are unsure about trusting ourselves. According to my theory, religion is a means of indirectly believing in ourselves by believing it is God who is providing us with the power to face our problems. There is a classic Indian metaphor from Kabirdas' couplets that summarize this concept of God and the meaning within very well. The term "कस्तूरी मृग" or "Kastoori mrig" is often used to describe that which is within, it refers to deer musk, which is a fragrant substance derived from a gland near the navel of a deer. This term is used because in Kabirdas' poetry deers are depicted running around in distress, constantly searching for the source of the fragrance they smell. Little do they know that in reality, the source is *within* them. Here the deer is meant to be a metaphor for man who is afflicted by the compulsion to find meaning without and addressing God as something that is external while really God is within us.

In addition to psychoanalysis, as introduced to me via "Ikigai: The Japanese Secret to a Long and Healthy Life", Morita therapy is another school of psychology about managing emotions developed by Shoma Morita. Morita explained the negative effects of obsessive thinking using a very suitable fable about a donkey tied to a post by a rope. As the donkey keeps walking around in circles in an attempt to be liberated, the more it is trapped and bound to the post. Similarly, we spiral down into the abyss of our own suffering, the more we obsess over thinking about it in hopes that somehow we are escaping from the problem. As mentioned earlier, Victor E. Fankl refers to this as "anticipatory anxiety" where phobias cause symptoms, which in turn produce more symptoms which cause phobias, it is an endless cycle of our anxiety perpetually tormenting us.

Shoma Morita is a Zen Buddhist, a culture with a variety of beautiful simple philosophies just like the one below about feelings:

If we try to get rid of one wave with another we end up with an infinite sea

Shoma Morita claims that emotions are natural and really the only thing we can do with them is to accept them, but I believe that transforming our emotions is what helps us achieve our true potential. I divide emotions into two groups which call "efficacious emotions" and "inefficacious" emotions. The goal is to convert inefficacious emotions into efficacious ones.

[See Efficacious Emotions in "Chapter Eight: Vantage" for more details]

Chapter Eight: Vantage

In my opinion, my greatest mental asset is my mild case of Bipolar Disorder and Multiple Personality Disorder. These "disorders" once, unbeknownst to me plagued my psyche. I was subconsciously puppeteered by my own subconscious. The thing with these disorders is that they don't mold your thoughts or start to transform what already exists. Rather it starts from scratch and generates a brand new mindset, a new separate means of thinking, new definitions for right and wrong. It was a little too much to handle for a teenage boy, sometimes it felt like there were loose switches scattered around the departments of decision making and the sub-departments of ethics and morality being flipped up and down by the devil and the angel. The whole situation was not a very productive addition to a prefrontal cortex which obviously isn't fully developed at this stage of human development.

Resorting to studying philosophy, theology and everything under it raised significantly more questions than they answered by exposing me to the branches of philosophy such as metaphysics, ethics, epistemology, and logic. Accompanied by all this were a plethora of concepts accompanied regarding everything from the fundamental nature of reality to the meaning of life. I guess the real reason I started to study philosophy was to make a better sense of my surroundings, and honestly, it helped. Over time I learned that there was an almost perfect correlation between observance and luck, awareness and opportunities. Being able to make astute observations allows one to look in the right places and from an abundance of angles to find meaning in their life.

At a certain point in my life, I did find myself becoming more and more stoic by the day with so much to contemplate, so much to feel, I had almost started feeling numb to emotions. True, sometimes we fail to manage negative energy and feelings but although it may be hard, one must learn to take agitation, fear, frustration, sadness, anger and what I call inefficacious responses and transform them efficacious responses such as diligence and conscientiousness to propel oneself towards their absolute potential.

The reason I actually dedicated time to think about responses and devise terms for good and bad ways to respond with emotions and transforming emotions was due to a quote by Lou Holtz I had recently read:

Life is ten percent what happens to you and ninety percent how you respond to it.

This one quote alone sums up everything I have said so far about responses and attitudes towards life. This time I want to phrase keeping an open mind a little differently, being like water. I can remember whether I heard it somewhere or if it was an original thought from when I was pouring myself a glass of water. Water is versatile it takes the shape of whatever it is put into, in a similar fashion, a fine person is such a person who can completely immerse themselves into any situation no matter what it is and "get a feel for it" from every one of its corners and seep into all its cracks and crevices to view it from every possible angle. This is not the only way to interpret versatility, the definition of versatility itself is very versatile in the sense that a person can be versatile in terms of their ability to cope with situations, perceive situations, etcetera.

Speaking of situations and attitudes I felt it was important to also include a few words about facing distressing situations and coping with mental illnesses and depression. Firstly, escape is never a justified coping mechanism, to prevent people from resorting to avoiding distressing situations and confronting people about their problems or confessing to certain things, I refer to the famous Buddha quote which goes like this:

Three things cannot be long hidden: The sun, the moon, and the truth

Therefore I say, do not suppress emotions because suppression is like throwing stuff into a volcano to prevent it from erupting unaware of the fact that that will only agitate it even more and make it erupt with even greater force and consume you with all you had thrown into it. This metaphor is not only applicable to individuals suppressing their emotions, but to parents suppressing their children too. Certainly, it is natural for a parent to be overprotective of their child, but as stated countless times previously, balance is key, and a child must be allowed a certain level of freedom. Speaking of parent-child relationships and truth, a quick note I'd like to add is about transparency. Transparency is the key to any healthy relationship along with (mutual) respect. There aren't any chapters that talk about the importance of parents thus I would like to include right here a very important point; parents are our living gods. A general rule of thumb for making good choices is to never do that which would hurt your parents and/or bring regret in retrospect. Always imagine that your parents are watching over your shoulders, witnessing every action.

I feel it is extremely important for problems to be addressed or at least for emotions to be allowed up to the surface level rather than being kept trapped deep inside. Catharsis can, after all, be greatly therapeutic. Usually, I try to think about what's the worst that could happen if I address negative feelings in front of an adult, it is not like they would get mad at you for going through bad times, they are experienced and they are sure to provide help. Usually problems do not even exist in the first place, it is important to get to their roots and understand what is really even causing them in the first place because sometimes problems do not even exist and we unnecessarily overcomplicate life for ourselves.

I like how simple the flowchart below depicts how to live a stress free life:

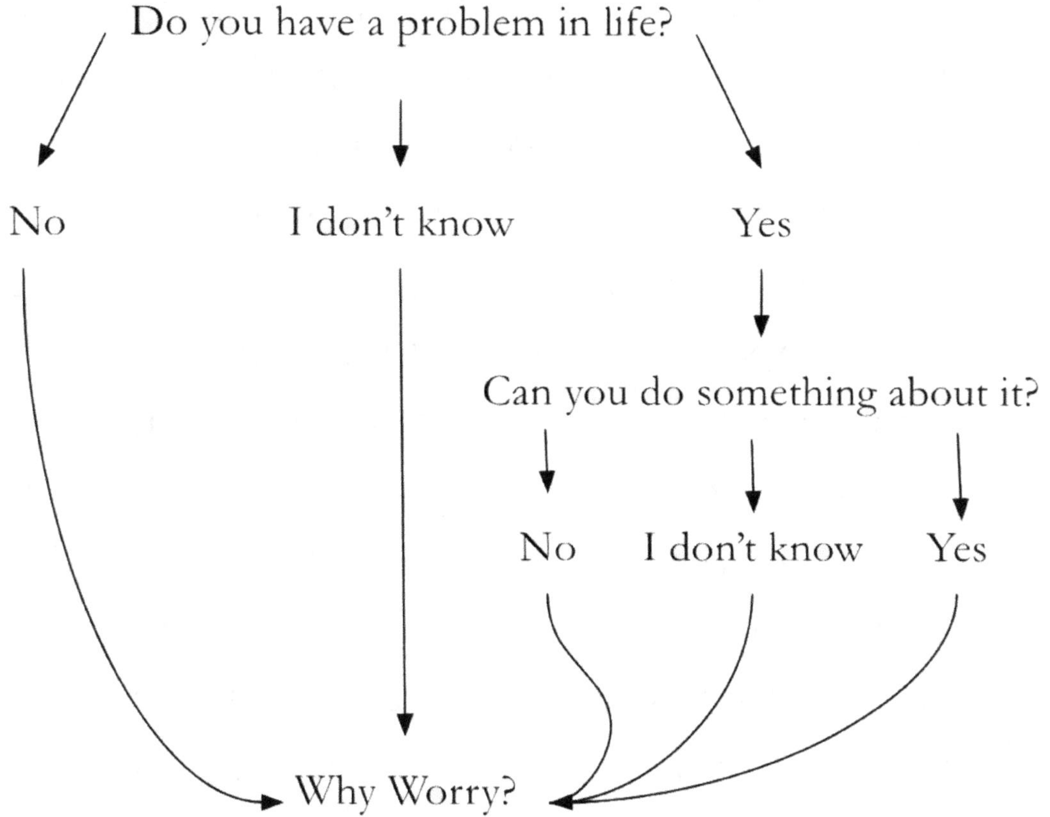

Of course life is not that simple and the greatest advice is to act with integrity, hope for the best, but be prepared for the worst.

Going back to managing emotions and efficacious vs inefficacious emotions, I call them efficacious and inefficacious responses because emotion is merely a response to a circumstance, it is up to us which emotions we allow to make their way to the surface. Emotions form deep in our subconscious, those who tend to be less self-aware tend to have less control over their emotions and inevitably give themselves more stress than they need. In my theory, all inefficacious responses have efficacious responses, responses that of course allow us to have a discharge of emotion and react to a scenario but more importantly, do so in a fashion that does not bring detriment to our mental state of mind. Instead, efficacious responses help us grow and therefore benefit from a situation. When we transform an inefficacious response into an efficacious response we are assigning meaning to it. Some examples of inefficacious responses and their efficacious counterparts are; sadness/frustration $\rightarrow$ motivation, and envy $\rightarrow$ inspiration/motivation.

The key point I'm attempting to convey here is that in any scenario one must have a good vantage point or in other words an open mind, the ability to have control over one's mind and view conflict from a different angle. On the grand scale of life for the prosperity of oneself and human civilization as a whole, everything must be interpreted via an open-mind, tolerant of all beliefs, views and opinion. So much comes down to perspective and learning to find positivity in everything. Our mindsets are our window into the world. Life goes on and things keep happening around us, but what matters is how we react to them. The same boiling water that softens the potato, hardens the egg. After all life is all about transforming all the struggles into something positive, if not positive, at least something meaningful.

Victor E. Frankl dedicates a section of his book talking about "A Case for Tragic Optimism". What should be understood by "a tragic optimism."? As Frankl writes; "in brief it means that 'one is, and remains, optimistic in spite of the 'tragic triad,' as it is called in logotherapy, a triad which consists of those aspects of human existence which may be circumscribed by: (1) pain; (2) guilt; and (3) death… allows for: (1) turning suffering into a human achievement and accomplishment; (2) deriving from guilt the opportunity to change oneself for the better; and (3) deriving from life's transitoriness an incentive to take responsible action.'''

Often during psychoanalysis and critical thinking situations of cognitive dissonance are created and personally I feel such instances are fantastic and have great benefits as they help you towards becoming an incisive thinker. John M. Keynes one said something that helps reinforce this idea of the importance of being able to think:

The difficulty lies, not in the new ideas, but in escaping from the old ones, which ramify, for those brought up as most of us have been, into every corner of our minds,

John M. Keynes was a true visionary and I feel it was so important that a figure like him existed, a person who finally does not live in the past but rather moves on with time.

Nihilism and Heresy

Many children of the new generation adopt a nihilistic outlook on the world. More and more people are becoming what one may call heretics, because more and more people are entering their years of youth. The time when people turn away from religion and stuff that does not make sense and it situated in this foggy grey area between known and unknown. Heretics listen to science, only to what they can really see, but they fail. To realize that rarely are things really as they seem. Essentially, adopting a nihilistic approach towards life strips life of any meaning, sure there is that aspect that such an approach to life burdens people with the responsibility to give life meaning but when many believe that religion was institutionalized to instill a sense of hope and comfort in people, why do so many renounce it. Perhaps it's just too complex, maybe it is due to concepts of right and wrong, and what it means to sin, some perceive religious laws as restrictive and simply wish to be liberated from it. Regardless I feel destiny is self-fulfilling when someone tries to exert their free-will and makes decisions to make something of their life, in my opinion, they are effectively fulfilling their destiny.

Foresight

They say hindsight is 20/20 as once a potential meaning has been actualized it exists in the past where it can be visited and remembered by never retrieved. Why don't we use this and past feelings of regret to make sure we simply don't make choices we will regret? As Victor E. Frankl says:

Live as if you were living for the second time and had acted as wrongly the first time as you are about to act now.

This is very similar to what my great-grandfather always told my grandmother; to begin with the end in mind and act with prudence.

He states in his book, "Man's Search for Meaning" that the opportunities to conduct ourselves responsibly and the potentialities to fulfill a meaning, are affected by the inevitable irreversibility of past choices. Frankl puts the actualization of a potential meaning as rescuing it into the past where it is safely delivered and deposited. He writes:

In the past, nothing is irretrievably lost, but rather, on the contrary, everything is irrevocably stored and treasured.

I feel this is a great way of imagining the past, putting what happens every second in this way really makes us rethink what choices we want to make and what potential meaning we want to actualize and deposit in the post for all of eternity.

Chapter Nine: Gears

Management is such an essential component of life, management of emotions, management of people and the management of society.

What would happen if society were mismanaged? What does that mean? To me, unity is the fundamental concept or goal that society (should) revolves around. To me, society is like intricate clockwork with people being the individual gears. Some gears may be bigger than others but every single one is equally as important and society can only function is all the gears work in harmony. The definition of a perfect society to me is a society where all power and rights are distributed equally, the closest we have come to this is (theoretical) communism, the problem is that utopian ideologies do not work in a dystopian world which is incompatible with such ideologies. I do not want to go too much into political science and the philosophy of politics but do want to briefly address what makes politics "messy". In my opinion, everything boils down to the fact that we are only human, it is merely the flaws of the mind that are referred to as human instinct, it is our greatest weakness. Our instincts are also coincidentally the one thing we tend to entwine into politics.

The fact that karma is a fundamental law of the universe that ensures balance will always be brought to a misbalanced, unfair society. Everything about life, human society, history is cyclic, it will never fail to correct that which needs correction, thus unity in the only means of attaining true, peace, justice, and socio-economic prosperity. Sure, It is merely human nature to be overwhelmed by power, corruption, greed and material desires. With great power comes great responsibility because power is unlike anything else, it is a dark mysterious force that corrupts unbeknownst to its bearer. Human nature and the limitations it causes to be manifested in the world of politics can best be explained by comparing it to the characteristics of a storm, a metaphor inspired by Seamus Heaney's, "Storm on the Island". Wind and natural disaster are inevitable, it is simply nature executing itself, although destructive, it is what brings balance, it is what restores. Likewise, the key element that often makes the fundamental nature of politics so convoluted is due to the role of human instinct and the means by which it impacts our decision making and effectively influences the manner in which we conduct politics. Usually, it isn't the strong winds of the storm that cause significant damage but rather it is the material objects that get caught in the storm which in this case refers to the entanglement of human instincts and material desires in matters that concern a purpose greater than oneself, a duty that must be performed for the welfare of society and human civilization. Politics. In the end, the only questions for humanity are; when will man stop corrupting power? when will man be united? when will society can be equal?

Love

They say love makes the world go round. That love is what the world needs, but it truly is a hard idea to grasp. I don't find myself qualified to really define anything here, I'd like to remind any readers that at the start I did state that this was originally meant for me to reflect upon and refine my philosophical ideals. Any claims I make do not have to be accepted as if they were derived from a doctrine, they are simply approaches to open ended enigmas.

It is important that we pay attention to love and try to display it whenever we can after all love unites us. Personally I try to treat others as if they were a part of me. Really I feel that the entire human race is one collective entity just a little confused about how remain united and at peace with itself. I often see other people as myself at different states. It is human nature to connect things to personal experiences and prior knowledge to better understand those things. When I see an angry person, I see myself in an angry state, I know that anger cannot fight anger because no person has fought with themselves because they were annoyed at the fact that they were angry. Anger subsides with time. When dealing with others I think of it as counselling myself because I find that there will always be a similar scenario I have faced and tackled.

The reason the world lacks love is because humans are impulsive and egocentric they quickly get angry at others because they believe the others are inferior to them. The problem is we blame things on others when in fact nothing is ever purely one person's fault, pre-existing circumstances may lead to a person making bad choices. Choices don't make themselves, they are either caused by certain triggers or are responses to previous choices. We just cannot tolerate our ego getting hurt.

The instance that drove me to the realization that the anger comes from within and that anger does not have to be my natural response was when I picked my phone and exclaimed "What do you want?!", I thought it was a friend but it was actually my father. It was at that moment that I realized that what I thought was my friend's call did not make me angry, the anger came from within and was due to other pre-existing emotions.

God created the Earth but we cut it up into countries. The belief that we are separate, inferior/superior is what further divides us. The world needs to be enlightened, it need people in it to spread love. All I ask from you is to spread love. Only then might we have a chance at a united world.

Chapter Ten: The Mind

Discussions revolving around the mind and things that hold pertinence to it such as psychological constructs have already occurred a multitude of times previously however I decided that it was imperative that I dedicate a chapter to discussing the incomprehensible power of the human brain. Notice that I utilized the word "brain" and am explicitly drawing attention to this decision. I did so to satisfy people who possess knowledge of psychology and are aware that the "brain" and "mind" are indeed two distinct entities that cannot be referred to interchangeably. This is where the philosophy of transcendence comes in which states that the greater being (God) is a transcendental being existent beyond the material universe, in a certain sense, liberated from physical reality and the laws that govern the universe that we reside in and is known to us. In an analogous manner, many argue that the mind is not a physical aspect of the brain, but rather an integrant of a greater transcendental world which is what gives birth to the abstract cognitive faculties of the mind consciousness, imagination, perception, thinking, judgment, language, and memory. I would certainly be pleased to go on having a pseudoscientific discussion about the mind but really the point I wished to make by providing some background on the mind and overcomplicating things we find simple such as imagination and thinking etcetera is that the human body is a marvel of nature and the mind is almost like its crown jewel.

The mind is an embodiment of possibility it is what bridges the gap between the principles of potentiality and actuality. The infinite capabilities of the mind provide us with the power to construct realities simply by indulging in a practice called believing.

It is hard for the average person to find happiness in spiritual and religious practices such as meditation and abstinence because they are considered boring or unsatisfying. The illusion of possession is one of the worst poisons yet we are materialistic creatures, this may be partly due to the fact that the human brain is hardwired to assign value to only that which is physical so it is almost natural for humans to be materialistic creatures. Speaking of value, recently I have written a lot about three specific terms in my journals; belief, meaning and value. This train of thought stemmed from my reading of George Orwell's, "Nineteen

Eighty-Four" which drove me to think of power and its origins, not just political power, any power including the power of a currency which really is just a piece of paper that we give value to by believing it has value. What is the role of belief in our lives and in the exhibition of reality as it is itself? As I contemplated this, it led me to think that value exists only when it is given, and that value and belief are intertwined. Things need value of some sort to be perceivable and thus become a component of reality. If belief is what gives rise to value and allows for its manifestation in material objects, abstract (metaphysical) concepts, etcetera, belief is the very foundation of reality.

Now I'm no expert but I will try my best to explain the differences between belief, meaning and value. It should be taken into consideration that this is merely my opinion.

Belief

I believe that belief is more abstract and that value can be perceived as the materialization of belief. Belief always emanates from the mind and is different for everyone, and is ever changing. Humans create beliefs and decide what they want to believe.

Meaning

Unlike belief, I believe that meaning is pre-determined by a greater being and is always the same. We may search for meaning and find something different to the true meaning assigned to us. Meaning is open to interpretation but remains constant unlike value and belief which are more dependent on each other and other external factors. Meaning is a part of predestiny.

Value

Value as defined earlier, is a realer form of belief, an actualized form of belief. I say this because belief can be associated with things and concepts that are not universally accepted and relates more to individual people. E.g.: I could all of a sudden say that I believe doorways are cursed, now that is not a universally recognized fact, it is a personal belief and therefore it does not really possess any value in the world. Value is more universal and is dependent on the number of people who give something value. E.g.: The value of a currency is dependent on the general population believing that a piece of paper with some ink and shiny ribbons can be worth hundreds of euros despite probably having less monetary value than a 2 euro coin. Value is like power, the government of a country has no power if the people of the country do not give the government power. In the same manner that power is collective, value is collective.

My motive to define belief, meaning and value was to present the thoughts that led to one of my greatest epiphanies from some while ago; everything is in the mind. This idea is tossed around way too much and this degrades the phrase's true value. To conclude this thought I will try to add value back into this phrase by elaborating upon how I realized that the mind is indeed everything. Upon reflecting on what is meant by everything stumbled upon the word, "reality". Reality is comprised of things we assign meaning and value to (living beings, material objects, abstract concepts), meaning and value are derived from belief. Belief is thus the foundation of reality as mentioned earlier. Since belief emanates from the mind, the mind alone is everything. Our mind is what creates our reality.

Materialism

Humans are materialistic creatures. Such (materialistic) instincts may be due to our primal instincts which were key to our survival. Everything about spirituality and religiousness the practices that come along with it essentially come down to being mindful. I do not know to call it simple or not but what it really is, is being aware of our actions and feelings, investigating why we make certain choices and growing from it is essentially what life is about and it is what will keep us going. Life is a journey of perpetual refinement and growth. This is why I say that it is important to make mistakes, after all, they are our greatest teachers, but only as long as we never repeat them, one can either stick by this, or choose to learn it the hard way.

Closing Remarks

In retrospect I must say that I grew much more as a person from writing this book than I did from the experience that initially drove me to write this book. This book was just as educational for me as I hope it was for you. For this journey I thank Ariadne for providing me a safe space to reflect, introspect, practice metacognition, and refine my thoughts, something I would recommend anyone to do. You can learn so much just from evaluating your thoughts. There is a thin line between reflecting and overthinking. Reflection is the same as overthinking but minus the anxiety and negativity, it is meant to be for growth, not catharsis.

Of course reading this book probably won't automatically solve all your problems as what is aims to do is help you develop and adopt a mindset similar to mine, a mindset which helped me recognize and really listen to the angel within me who guides me through everything. My book aims to help me help you help yourself because god helps those who help themselves and others around them.

Some may argue that philosophy often oversimplifies life and that there are many other factors such as political, environmental, historical, societal, and economic factors that impact the quality of life and one's ability to live it to the fullest. The beauty of philosophy is that despite everything it can help people appreciate what they have and develop a better attitude towards life.

Yes the world is unfriendly, and although this book may seem like it is trying to make you soft hearted compassionate people with strong morals who will be cheated over and over in a world that is overwhelmed with corruption, I want you to realize that this book aims to do exactly the opposite. The goal is to be a strong hearted fighter with strong morals. In the real world sometimes lying is inevitable and lying is not always wrong, after all as mentioned earlier, everything is relative, it all depends on the context. Sometimes it is necessary to lie, to raise your voice and do things that are discouraged in this book, it just that with the power to hurt comes a lot of responsibility. Sometimes seemingly immoral actions are justified and confusing things like this is what complicates court cases and legal decisions. The key is to be balanced and know when to exhibit certain emotions and be compassionate but know to not let anyone take advantage of that compassion and kindness.

Once again I would like to thank my family for all their love and support. I would also like to thank my friends especially Jared and Maher who expressed overwhelming enthusiasm and helped me in this endeavour. Thank you Maher for helping me edit some of this and thank you so much Jared for leading me to re-read "Man's Search for Meaning" for the second time after which I took away way more than I did the first time.

Thank you Mamma for making me realize that nothing ever ends unless you make it end, that life is what you make it, and most importantly, that it's all about your attitude towards life. Perhaps the most important message I want to convey is that it is never the end. Where something ends, something new begins, what goes up must fall down, and what falls will bounce, the intensity of that bounce is dependent on our attitude towards life and ability to cope with loss and adversity.

- Arav Sri Agarwal

Bibliography

Frankl, Viktor E. Man's Search for Meaning; an
   Introduction to Logotherapy. A Newly Rev. and
   Enl. Ed. of From Death-Camp to Existentialism.
   Translated by Ilse Lasch. Pref. by Gordon W.
   Allport. Beacon Press, 1968.

Heaney, Seamus. Death of a Naturalist. Faber
   and Faber, 1969.

Miralles, Francesc. Ikigai - the Japanese Secret
   to a Long and Happy Life. Cornerstone, 2017.

Prabhupāda A. C. Bhaktivedanta Swami.
   Bhagavad-gītā as It Is. Bhaktivedanta
   Book Trust, 1997.

Prabhupāda A. C. Bhaktivedanta Swami. The
Science of Self Realization: Articles
from Back to Godhead Magazine. The
Bhaktivedanta Book Trust, 2015.

Philosophy Stack Exchange. "Are there
philosophical antecedents to each of
Newtons three Laws of Motion?."
Philosophy Stack Exchange. 16 Jun.
2012. Web. 21 Nov. 2019. <https://
philosophy.stackexchange.com/
questions/2998/are-there-philosophical-
antecedents-to-each-of-newtons-three-
laws-of-motion>

Romain Noir. "The Principle Of Polarity | Romain
Noir." *Romainnoir.net*. 31 Dec. 2017. Web. 25 Dec.
2019. <https://www.romainnoir.net/the-
principle-of-polarity/>

Russell, Bertrand. A History of Western
Philosophy. Simon & Schuster, 2005.

Stanford University. "Newton's Three Laws of Motion." Ccrma.stanford.edu. 30 Oct. 2019. Web. 21 Nov. 2019. <https://ccrma.stanford.edu/~jos/pasp/Newton_s_Three_Laws_Motion.html>

Walters, J. Donald. Little Secrets of Happiness. Crystal Clarity Publishers, 1994.

Walters, J. Donald. Little Secrets of Success. Crystal Clarity Publishers, 1994.

Walters, J. Donald. Secrets of Self-Acceptance. Crystal Clarity Publishers, 1993.